By Dinah Livingstone

Poetry Pamphlets:
Beginning (1967)
Tohu Bohu (1968)
Maranatha (1969)
Ultrasound (1974)
Prepositions and Conjunctions (1977)
Love in Time (1982)
Glad Rags (1983)
Something Understood (1985)
St Pancras Wells (1991)
Poetry Books:
Saving Grace (1987)
Keeping Heart (1989)
Second Sight (1993)
May Day (1997)
Time on Earth: Selected and New Poems (1999).
Edited:
Camden Voices Anthology 1978-1990 (1990)
Work: An Anthology (1999)
Prose:
Poetry Handbook for Readers and Writers (1992)
The Poetry of Earth (2000)

Her Translations Include:
Poetry:
Poems, Lorca and John of the Cross; *Nicaraguan Mass (Misa Campesina),*
Carlos Mejía Godoy; *Nicaraguan New Time,* Ernesto Cardenal; *Anthology
of Latin American Poets in London,* (part:); *Dawn Hunters and other Poems,*
Roberto Rivera-Reyes (part); *The Nicaraguan Epic,* Carlos & Luis Enrique
Mejía Godoy and Julio Valle-Castillo; *The Music of the Spheres,* Ernesto
Cardenal; *Prayer in the National Stadium,* María Eugenia Bravo Calderara;
Poets of the Nicaraguan Revolution.(anthology: trans. & ed.); *Life for Each,*
Daisy Zamora; *Nosotras: Poems by Nicaraguan Women* (anthology: trans.
and ed.); *Mother Tongues* (MPT 17 anthology: part).
Prose:
Nature and Grace, Karl Rahner; *In the Kingdom of Mescal,* Georg Schäfer;
The Truth is Concrete, Dorothee Sölle; *The Poor Sinner's Gospel,* Wilhelm
Weitling; *The Tupamaros,* Alain Labrousse; *The Desert is Fertile,* Helder
Camara; *Love,* Ernesto Cardenal; *Jesús of Gramoven,* A. Pérez Esclarín; *We
are like Dreamers,* Walter Beyerlin; *Death and Life in Morazán,* M. López
Vigil; *Companions of Jesus: The Murder and Martyrdom of the Salvadorean
Jesuits,* Jon Sobrino; *Moses,* Luis Alonso Schökel; *Our Cry for Life,* María
Pilar Aquino; *Carlos, Now the Dawn's No Fond Illusion,* Tomás Borge;
Angels of Grace, Anselm Grün; *We Will Not Dance on our Grandparents'
Tombs: Indigenous Uprisings in Ecuador,* Kintto Lucas; *Zapatista Stories,*
Subcomandante Marcos.

PRESENCE

PRESENCE

Dinah Livingstone

KATABASIS

First published on October 6th 2003,
William Tyndale's day,
by KATABASIS
10 St Martin's Close, London NW1 0HR (020 7485 3830)
katabasis@katabasis.co.uk
www.katabasis.co.uk
Copyright © Dinah Livingstone 2003
Printed by CLE Print, Media House, Burrel Road, St Ives,
Huntingdon PE27 3LE (01480 465233)
Typeset in-house mainly in 12 point Garamond.
Front and back cover paintings: Anne Mieke Lumsden
Frontispiece drawing:
Ash tree with Sparrow by Anne Mieke Lumsden

ISBN 0 904872 39 4
Trade Distribution: Central Books
99 Wallis Road
London E9 5LN
(020 8986 4854)
ISBN: 0904872 39 4

British Library Cataloguing in Publication Data:
A catalogue record for this book is available
from the British Library.

ACKNOWLEDGMENTS

Some of these poems have appeared in the magazines *Acumen, Exmoor Review, Frogmore Papers, Interpreter's House, London Magazine, Poet's Voice,* and in the anthologies *For Arnold with Love,* edited by John Lucas (Shoestring Press, Nottingham 2001); *Selected Poems of the United Kingdom,* edited by Patricia Oxley (Spiny Babbler, Kathmandu 2002); *In the Company of Poets,* edited by John Rety (Hearing Eye, London 2003).

Katabasis is grateful to Rockingham Press for permission to reprint eight poems from the 'New Poems' section of Dinah Livingstone's *Time on Earth: Selected and New Poems* (Rockingham Press, Ware 1999).

Many thanks to my proof readers, Helen Barrett, Grace Livingstone, Zoe Livingstone, and Dilys Wood.

CONTENTS

1. LONDON AND COUNTRY

2. MEXICO

3. PEOPLE AND OCCASIONS

1

LONDON AND COUNTRY

PRESENCE

To Cecily who taught us to think about presence

Prologue: Absent-minded

Frequently distracted by anxiety,
I footle checking, planning this or that,
while traffic, clanking plumbing makes me fret,
or phoning, moaning, mainly inwardly.
I wonder what's the point of poetry,
what this lonely life itself is all about.
I wander restlessly and cannot write,
absent from me with anything to say.
But who can give the answer to it all?
Claiming no special knowledge, let me reach
somewhere, an insight, find word to follow word
which gets that out, is adequate to tell
you, delicately connect in common speech,
humbly presenting myself by being heard.

The Intensity of the Geranium

At seven when I wake the room is dark.
Slowly on pink curtain the geranium is outlined,
its upsprawling, pungent, jagged leaves defined
by the returning light, precise and stark,
its shape more present as the colour is still black,
but now a rosy opalescence strokes my mind
as through the chink a cloud-puffy kind
of sunrise peeps with morning's hopeful ache.
I have felt so futile and alone,
pottered unproductively for days
wondering if I'd done all I'd ever do.
The geranium is quite still though it has grown
huge and its intensity impresses this sunrise
with its self-stress, promising mine back too.

House

Beyond repair the window's rotten frame,
and now its bottom bar has fallen down.
For the thirty-sixth year the privilege has been mine
to spend and tend this old house in my name.
I know my luck but sometimes just the same
I get tired of all the traffic roaring down
and all the uglier side of Camden Town:
is it time to retire to somewhere trim and tame?
But the fabric of the house is inextricable
from my own make-up, my life, my work, my poetry.
My children grew up here, the last from birth.
I'm not a stranger here: my history's physical.
Rot and renewal saga of organic memory,
not a neat plot, holds my home on earth.

St Martin's Gardens

These gardens for the overflow of graves
from St Martin's in the Fields are our lung,
our public open space; they now belong
to ghosts and many local London lives.
Dappled sunlight through the plane tree leaves,
shadows of municipal railings flung
aslant the path, my tiny daughter climbing
the monstrous slide, the kindly gardener saves
my naughty four-year-old lost son,
now long ago, but in the atmosphere
of this between-the-housebacks little park,
the back of many minds, a village green
in Camden, like the tombs they stay here,
though still with all their future fresh to make.

Refugees

They lock you up to keep you out of sight.
They keep you out so you do not disturb
our cosy normal busy days, but herb
of grace is rue, sorrow bitter to bite.
We see your faces everywhere, your desperate
crawl through rat-infested sewage pipe,
leap across lethal rail; nothing can curb
that urgent dare drown, burn or suffocate.
I didn't invite you but you've got to me;
I can't exclude your presence from my mind,
roaring for justice or a still small voice.
You won't allow me my complacency.
You infiltrate my idleness with scent
of a sage order, taste of common peace.

Love and Death

The bliss of being together made the pain
of parting that acute. Like being dead
and howling it alive along the blood,
the loss most intimate leaves most alone.
Feels less than half a human to be one,
for love transformed the couple that it made,
though halves return to wholes and hurts recede
and simple pleasure bubbles up again.
These are the unbitter who survive
with memories that are strong but do not harm,
who still enjoy life's game though they grow old.
Absence and presence mingle: they receive
a bonus, but when birds sing in spring, that calm
is jolted by a pang that dreads the cold.

Christmas Carol

We're singing carols in this ancient church.
It's Anglican and rather high, it seems:
the Real Presence with its red light gleams.
For seventeen centuries St Pancras much
honoured in this place, heroic boy
martyr against the Beast: we greet our dead
and Jesus born the soul and body of his God
(idea that lived and died but not that way).
We recall the story and the man
and his mother come to mind tonight,
though *hoc est corpus* can't be swallowed whole.
But you are singing gloriously. I turn
and smile at your pink cheeks and woolly hat
rhyming sublime with cherubime for real.

Beyond

Is there a presence beyond the cloud of unknowing?
Can it be pierced by a strong spear of love,
which passes like a plane through murk to the sun above?
No, not this, not that, is where I'm going.
Is there someone speaking at the heart of being,
wording the world and everything alive,
uncreated author of all we are and have?
No. That is not what I'm hearing, seeing.
Brightness beyond dark, silence beyond speech, absence
of interruption hold the moment still,
the instant of pure energy to contemplate
what is always flowing, all at once,
make sense and love, yes, urgently to feel
warm with this life, right here where I sit.

Energy

And sometimes like those ancient bikes that jolt
suddenly into a different gear,
shudder uncontrollably and roar
from the deep wellspring kept sealed
with an oak lid and massive iron bolt,
because it is the dangerous human core
of undifferentiated energy, that is pure
rage and love, raw stuff of life revealed.
Without this partner stillness cannot dance,
who can turn ugly like a drunken brawl,
who is unstoppable transgression.
And is the fluff-beaked building blue-tit's tense
chittering, tight ash bud's first frill
of tender green. The poetry is in the passion.

Millfield Lane

When Keats met Coleridge here in Millfield Lane
hard by the next pond up from the Ladies' Pond,
did the Highgate sage feel death in the hand
he clasped and pity the promising, younger man?
Another April now I see the trees return
they might have seen, oak, sycamore, and stand
ravished by the giants' delicate flowers, on ground
where they stood talking under this fresh green.
New-burst from sticky buds, horse-chestnut leaves
droop like unfledged birds until they spread.
Rabbits. Cowslips in a sunny ditch:
like the poets, these still share our lives
as fellow Londoners, interconnected,
re-affecting, making each meeting rich.

Bunhill Fields

In my exchanges every land shall walk.
Spring fig-leaves shine, the pink horse chestnut blooms.
Bluebells cluster round the leaning tombs.
I stand in Bunhill Fields and nod to Blake
as workers picnic in their lunchtime break.
This dream of London as Jerusalem
is of a fruitful city which has room
for all kinds of folk. They are what wake
and widen it with other stories to tell.
I'm glad the conker blossoms aren't all white
and many shapes and colours make a garden.
Refugees, you are welcome. I hope you will
feel at home here, won't have to fight
too many fools, become flowers of London.

St Giles Cripplegate

Where St Giles Cripplegate squats in the Barbican,
I summon Milton needed at this hour.
Getting and spending we still waste our power.
The City is ambivalently golden
dark in thrall to the dark idol Mammon.
Help us to save free conscience from the paw
of hireling wolves whose gospel is their maw,
as human worth contests with hell for London.
Your Samson's answer was to smash it all,
destroying himself and bystanders besides.
Can there be no other way to change
the polis? Is another world possible
with new awareness like a seed that sprouts
from compost into something huge and strange?

Clerkenwell Green

'Know that lack of fellowship is death.
Fellowship is life,' hedge-priest John Ball
told William Morris and these old words still
inspire a fresh year's May Day march to breathe
the heady air of Clerkenwell, strong with
that long-fermented hope like real ale.
A troop of children clothed in red recall
Kurdish names of dead and living both
present today, and many other tongues
babble a common spirit. Trafalgar Square
Morris imagined is where the change began.
The procession shambles towards it. Shouts and songs
yearn to hear weird news from everywhere
of Earth as comfortable for everyone.

Tota Simul

Wanting to see, to hold infinity
in the palm of your hand, the mind's scope no less
than beauty so old, so new, uttering logos
keeping all present in eternity,
all at once, with love, whose sight is simply
overflowing spirit, ache for peace,
desire of nations for enjoyment, justice
somehow, for all at once, equally.
God was the encoded name of that unwritten,
unachieved, but which can happen nowhere else
but here, but now, will never be complete.
Local acts think global, having seen
the sheen of that totality in each little
sand grain, each poem saying not yet.

The Quietness of the Peacock Feathers

Home in the evening after another day,
I want my supper and a glass of wine,
grateful for a good digestion.
I'm feeling tired, mortal ordinary.
Despite friends and neighbours, a bit lonely
at odd moments, praying my grown-up children
will be all right, nothing dreadful happen,
I love them so much and feel very lucky.
I sit in my usual place and read or dream,
nod off to television, then wake up
and contemplate the peacock feathers' shadow
on the ceiling, catch their emerald gleam.
Now at dead of night words stop,
unwound to one syllable, just O.

History

My youngest daughter
who grew up to study history
phones to say that for her conference
she needs the Penguin *May Day Manifesto*
Raymond Williams 1967.
She can't find a copy anywhere in London.
I tell her to look through the dusty books
high on the shelves in the passage.
Dad took some but maybe it's still there.

Like sunrise she arrives in the early morning
pink from her bike with her bright hair.
With a rush of energy she mounts the steps.
Still in pyjamas I dither below.
Some of the shelves are double-stacked,
paperbacks are falling to bits.
Triumphant she picks out the small red one,
descends with a big grin, kisses my cheek
and is gone. Now we are told
those far-off dialectics of liberation
are an outmoded epic that might as well
be Beowulf and Grendel. 'Wasted', 'history'
in Yank gangster dialect meaning dead.

I remember reading poems with Madge Herron
at that conference in the Round House
and Oliver Bernard went to Paris
to gather and translate the graffiti:
L'imagination au pouvoir! –
Wollstonecraft's true fire stolen from heaven.
Well, now that's history dead and buried.

But as I watch this new generation
climbing a rickety step ladder
to reclaim what it seeks today,
I hear grand narrative whisper the words
of Great-Heart: Yet you see I am alive!

Voices

Tired body, brain occluded,
darkness and deep sleep fell.
Shadows and voices visited
intermittently and faded.
Then on a summer morning
I wake to the heavenly sense
of earthly energies restored,
new light pouring in,
another day, another chance.
The night is over.

In the interval before I have my tea
consciousness drifts in and out.
I remember the dead. Some familiar
make their presences felt –
my mother in her New Look dress
wafting out for the evening her fleshy
love-and-death hyacinth scent,
my father bellowing across two fields:
'Bring on that bucket, Di!'
Yes, most of all certain tones,
things that they said.

I think of all those others
I never met but whose words I have,
particular poems that have meant the most
and formed me as I now am.
Lines float into my head,
sound-coracles leaving a voice-wake
on my mind.

And I hear voices of the living,
some now in other places,

some I saw yesterday and will see today.
Selves intermingling. Intimacies.
All those conversations, words,
are the web that sustains me,
the hammock that rocks me
into this new breakfast.
Even more intrinsic, they are
the waking stuff I am made of.

Yesterday I was translating and it was hard.
I hear Tyndale, who was the first
to translate the Bible from the original
Greek and Hebrew – and they burnt
your pocket book New Testaments
smuggled to England in bales of cloth.
Arrested you asked for a candle
in your winter prison. Then they burnt you
near the site of what is now Brussels Airport.
I hear your lucid English phrases I know so well.
Let there be light, you said,
and I see it streaming in through the window.

Cold

I open the sash
to put out my breakfast crusts
on the sill for the bluetits –
shyer than sparrows,
more of an honour in London,
yellow breasted, delicate bluebell heads –
who visit me this winter
when I sit at my second floor window
processing words.
A fierce December gust freezes my face.
It's eleven o'clock in the morning,
still sullen and dark. It looks
as if it might stay like that all day.
I shudder and shut fast.

No sign of the little birds
who cheer me when they come,
darting in like a bit of a poem
I must catch sight of before,
in a flash, they're away with their triumph
of toast crumbs for comfort.
I hope they'll survive the cold,
and through dreary January, February,
continue to scatter their poetic
alightings, swift guerrilla heart raids,
which keep that sudden blessing unawares
alive in a lonely frozen season.

This poem was written before the decimation of London sparrows,
to whom I apologise for taking them for granted on page 27.

Day

The York stone pavements are still wet
but after so much rain the sun
this morning is shining again
making the exuberant yellow and rose
in the print on my door of Blake's *Glad Day*
self-evident. I've decided to stay in bed,
try to get rid of this cough.

After a shower, in a clean nightgown
I am deliciously warm. As well as outbursts
of sparrows outdoors I hear builders
making a brushing sound
with occasional laughter, busy working,
which adds a bit extra to my enjoyment
of feebleness this day off.

The sunlit plane tree leaves are waving.
You sent me flowers and the little pinkish
kind of Michaelmas daisies are making the room
smell sweet. The tang of satsuma I open
comforts my rough throat.
A bundle of sensations, what,
I wonder idly, am I more than these?

The answer is immediate:
I am who I am.
For as far back as I can remember
even when I was five
I've always been sure of that.

I am who I am
was God's name for himself
in the burning bush,

glad day's energy pouring out
being, speaking, loving

but in my self-awareness
earthly, even when feeble
human form divine I share,
so that when I securely say I am
I conjugate you are.

SEED

New Grass

Come Ash Wednesday grass must be resown
that disappeared in winter from this plot
of London earth. Pale seeds sit tight,
a spread for birds, look too dead to open.
Dreary February week on week goes by.
The first green hairs are frail beyond belief,
gather to a haze the eye fears is illusive,
as long March snorts and sings out wilfully.
By Easter alleluia it has risen,
indeed, it has become a little lawn.

Enchanter's Nightshade

From what dark wood
did you travel to Camden Town
to squat my little garden?
There you multiplied,
flourished in the gloomy places
where not much else would grow,
conjuring from deep shadow
heartshapes, white-sketched faces.
With the green leaves of survivors
flock your lacy flowers.

.

Nearer

I am glad there is no God here
requiring attention in this garden.
Just the garden itself, which does
and I who do.

When I praise that buddleia
sprouting from the crumbling wall
for being a tough old Londoner
who hangs on even there, perfuming
with its wavy long-tailed blossom
the hard-working air,
and attracting butterflies and bees,
I do not expect it to listen
or answer back.

I don't want a supernatural
interlocutor when I admire
the delicate ferny herb robert
proliferate wildly this summer.
I imported one plant from a hedgerow
years ago for an uprooted Chilean poet
coming to tea in this same garden,
to welcome him with an English weed
called by his name. Starry pinkish flower
and human voice and memory
are ample.

The early morning sun is up
and over the roof tops.
Buttercups tangle at my feet, brilliant
among long grasses beginning to seed.
Hollyhocks steeple above me.
I wish their leaves were not so rusty

but their bells peel with pale pure colours,
sweet ethereal music of earth,
whereas the sparrows' chatter is domestic:
London wildlife at work at home.

After a bad time of fear
and seemingly endless anxious distraction
I return to myself,
sit still with everything here.
A kind of poem starts to form.
I am glad there's no God in this garden,
though the poem seems like a kind of prayer.

Where I Belong

St John's Garden, Regent's Park

'Thou hast made us for thyself
and our hearts are restless
till they rest in thee.' – AUGUSTINE

Yes, I suffer that restlessness.
I always have, but no,
I will not address myself
to a god I don't believe.
But where can I go
for words of eternal life?

There is no eternity –
duration of that which does not change –
so where amid the changes and chances
of this fleeting world
set my heart? Can that be found?

Actually, Augustine, you were right
that seeking perfect circumstances,
the perfect man, the perfect place,
provides no solution.
Life in time flows on.

Fleeting, yes, but now and again. Today
by half past two on a mid-winter afternoon
the sun in this sodden garden
is beginning to set. Pale gold falls
on the rosemary's few blue flowers.
A chaffinch flits about the espaliered limes.

Where is peace? Not
in the waddling pigeon or bounding squirrel,
not even the clean silhouette
of the crow in the naked pear tree,
who will soon flap away.

Not in stasis. Not in possession
but belonging. Not
in that or this, but all of it
and me as part of it, sat on a wet seat,
haloed in earthlight,
which before teatime will be gone.

Gorse

Sat at Minsmere in May,
I feel the air so soft,
I smell the new-sweet earth.
Gorse dazzles my eyes,
each individual root
prickles up to its skyward shape,
bush upon bush outpouring
its cornucopia of gold,
till defining my left horizon
they tip over the crumbling cliff
into global blue – a boat
from here might sail anywhere.

Briefly a green hairstreak
visits the blossom beside me,
which wafts, exotic for Suffolk,
a distinct whiff of coconut.

Grey

The willow is soft grey not silvery
whose leaves move gently in almost no breeze.
Its shape's a beautiful huge skyward oval
but without the sun I do not feel it.
The close grey sky is a heavy blanket
clamming my skin with a slight dull sweat.
The grey light is clear and all the greens
distinct in this orchard where apples plop
separately from time to time or the air
is interrupted by a grey pigeon fluttering
as it alights on the willow.
The Sunday morning church bell tolls
slowly over the flat fields.
Few follow it and I will not.

Where I sit I am not comfortable
and flies annoy me. Acutely I see and hear
but feel little, only know
grey is the necessary endurance
the in-between of neither sun nor rain
all the days of keeping on believing,
looking, listening carefully,
keeping my wits about me,
just keeping on, without recognition,
without blessing or reward
of any transfiguring golden vision
to rend the heavens and come down.

Rooted

1

Under a sky today in constant motion
I rest on my way up the combe,
the last fold in these hills
before they drop sheer to the sea,
whose violet, green and grey,
thrift-pink and sheep's-bit blue
keep altering.

The bell heather on top dazzles,
empurples me as I sit still,
with my wild-woman crown of hair
flapping pale-brown against my face
and matching the taller hairy grasses,
whipped by the same wind
across the heather's giant cranial curve.

I hear the rose-breasted stonechats
and watch the little black-tailed stoats,
active as the breeze about their business
among the loose tumbled pebbles
down the combe's flank. They run about
unconcerned by me, who for them
am now the hill.

2

Next morning after a violent storm
I climb the path to Culbone through the wet wood.
A gap occurs and I look back across the bay
to Hurlstone where I sat yesterday,

the curve of the coast and the curve of the hill
together shockingly beautiful.

Green-clad and dripping like the trees
I trudge on. Mossy oaks,
ash, hawthorn, hazel, rowan,
birch, holly, chestnut, beech,
sycamore and more all thrive
and tangle down the deep romantic chasm.
I notice laurel and think planting
and sure enough the path leads
under a ghostly arch and through a little tunnel
but the house these once approached is now abandoned.

A sudden wispy ground mist has crept down
and further arches form before my eyes
luring to imaginary fairy palaces
but these prove to be trees.
Now the sun dapples through
and raindrops glisten everywhere.
The magic forest shimmers in its primal potency,
holds me rooted and in thrall.

I reach Culbone, rest in the tiny church,
see most of the gravestones are Reds and Richards.
Up at Silcombe and neighbouring Ash Farm
(where the person from Porlock allegedly
interrupted Coleridge, who had walked this same way)
Mrs Richards and Mrs Richards her cousin
still offer bed and breakfast to the traveller.

Counting Sparrows

Sparrows were two a penny
and hard to count as the hairs on your head.
I remember how they used to flock
cheekily for crumbs from the cafe tables
outdoors in Regent's Park,
and what a racket they made
congregated in a bush
like the chapel of an enthusiastic sect –
cockney sparrows they were called,
such common birds.

Suddenly they went.
It was as if London's bird spirit,
its indigenous *nagual* or *chulel*
had abandoned it.
Who would expect to mind so much
their sad small absence?

Last week I saw three in a tree
and yesterday in breezy April sun
I sat at Kenwood and watched
a couple pecking at the gravel.
'Glad to see you back,' I said,
'please increase again. Now I count you
because you are so few.'

Nagual and *Chulel* are Mexican indigenous words for guardian animal spirits.

October 2001

War came. Bombs fell again.
Poor people try to flee,
clutching their ragged children,
towards winter without food.
They throng my eyes and mind
with helpless responsibility.
Fear of attack on London.
My dearest, beware the tube,
the fireball, seeping poison.

Meanwhile, on Hampstead Heath,
an autumn spurt of growth,
fresh brilliance in the grass
from spongy turf, my step more
elastic in the noble presence of trees,
each shape quintessentially distinct,
full dressed in waving leaves
becoming radiant before they fall.
Life's sweetness aches the urgency of peace.

Brink

Past the lookout point
with its mock fortification,
the sheer cliffs turn the corner
with a footpath barely wide enough
for sheep's deft, cloven hooves,
let alone a solid boot.
One step and you tumble
to a rough sea of confusion,
a turbulent, sinuous subplace
where the sobbing never stops
and all the woes of the world
weigh down to become
indistinguishable, beyond help,
almost beyond hope, with what little
is left of a self to battle
for a foothold regained
on firm ground.

Shape

I watch a graceful group of winter birch,
dappled brown and silver trunks
whose twiggy filigree red tops
gently finger the sunny sky
pianissimo. Then two walkers pass
conversing in local cockney
on the folly of war. I hear
their mouths form vowels,
typical labio-dental fricatives,
glottal stops, to make meaning, feeling
sound-shapes flowing like the silent
music of the outlined trees.

Beyond the static monolith,
over the oak's crown,
crows keep circling, settling,
each sharp black individual
convolving a moving pattern.
The rainbow's evanescent colours
interflow. Those beautiful young people
have grown from infant bodies
and are the same and not the same.
A loved face reappears, rhythm-reflected
in lapping water, dissolves, as sun goes in
and shapes shine only now and then.

As well as worse possibilities,
trying to set days, years, a life
in order, to become what is wanted,
has to confront the more humdrum
too tight shipshape, sheepish conformity,
slipshod *accidie*, that scupper the scope,
dull the sheen. That which

may have escaped, shun you,
nevertheless, gleams interstitially.

A grand narrative history
grows obsolete, needs re-imagining
with hope for the human race
that is the same and not the same.
Fundamentalism hates free growth,
as bound feet become misshapen,
trapped minds and spirits rigid,
murdered bodies shapeless lumps of meat.

Splendor formae, beauty so old and so new,
burns in the breast, and the instant caught
in a song sung, a still photo, a kiss,
belongs to earth's musical living process,
with new poems that go on being written
out of the *tohu* and *bohu* of dreams
as long as language survives,
so that people talk to each other
and mean it, grace of salsa and tango,
birdflight, treescape, opening celandine
on which the sun has shone, all
shift, rest, swift, slow, breathing or
breathless, organic, daring and fallible.

Ygdrasil

Ygdrasil in Camden Town,
uptwisting trunk great sycamore,
from my terrace I greet you early,
your crown curves so generously
against the new day's sky.
The rising sun lights your big body
and strikes the spiral iron fire escape
on the brick flats to your left,
so that its shadow shapes a double helix,
solid and ephemeral, as London wakes.
I look out over sheds, which gardeners
are about to visit to get their tools,
to where you stand in the park.
Soon a few old drunks will come
to sit on the tombstone at your foot,
argue politics with alcoholic logic,
scuffling from time to time.
Meanwhile, from the main road,
the muffled rush-hour roar picks up –
wildlife active to survive –
as, some still half asleep,
they thrust their way to work.

Ygdrasil, late afternoon
the sun comes round behind you
so that your leaves are now translucent.
I gaze from my terrace wrought-iron chair
surrounded by reddening autumn vines –
so many and such sweet grapes this year;
for me, much stress, frustration
but I've done some difficult work
I'm glad about. A resting body now
I nod to the delicate little cyclamen

in their big pots of plain earthenware
and sip pale yellow wine.
I look up. Ygdrasil,
I see your glory in the golden light.
You have clothed the sun in living green.
Breaking through it dazzles me.
I am in the heart of London and remember
Blake saw an angel
in a tree at Peckham Rye.

At 3 a.m. I wake in darkness
troubled by slithering anxieties
shifting between the global and domestic,
confusing images, noises of war.
I go out on the terrace and I see
stars muted by the crowding city
yet still their heavenly multitude.
Most of the houses round me are asleep.
Perhaps tonight in one of those dark rooms
a new life will be conceived.
Just the occasional lit window.
Maybe someone battling on with work
or woken too like me.
Over Ygdrasil,
complete with mountains visible,
the full moon beams down
silvering your black profile,
your strong presence like a ghost,
overflowing me with stillness and the sense
of Earth as a body needing peace,
herself a modest sphere in space
turning towards new day.

HEARTWORK

Response

'Work of seeing is done,
now do heartwork.' – RILKE, *Turning Point (Wendung)*

Work of seeing's never done:
greeting sorrel's reddened seeds,
flowering grasses mauve to brown,
all the other pleasant weeds.
Let not listening ever cease:
streams of water rushing down,
subtlest tones of speaking voice,
winter robin trilling on.

Intertwining in a web,
heartwork isn't *after* sight.
Waking senses, dreams in sleep,
both continue day and night.
Grasp, receive, each plays a part,
male and female principle.
World and wit with open heart
make the individual soul.

Rhythm Father

He rode hard, won races, black silk, pink cap.
Recklessly brave, winter on winter
he would fall and break at least his collar bone
but still rode on, jumping broad brooks,
huge cut-and-laid hedges.
An Englishman, he loved the country,
horn music on a frosty morning,
distrusted the word intellectual.
But he would encourage his small daughter,
after a hot bath at the end of the day,
to recall every detail of it, each path,
gate, fence (look out for wire),
the trees in the wood, flowers, animals,
each bird heard or seen, and tell the story.
The word poetry made him uneasy.
Master of the Blackmore Vale, perhaps
he wasn't keen on Thomas Hardy
but he loved rhythms and rhymes.
'Over the fence goes Sunny Jim.
Force is the food that raises him!'
he would bellow, or drone on a monotone:
'Love's a farce, sitting on your arse,
all by yourself in the moonlight.'
He adored the excited shape of the shout:
'Five to four the field!
Go back, boy, and give the horse
a very small feed of corn indeed!'
He shouted at his children too
and terrified them, later confessed
he was so frightened at being yelled at
in the Navy, but thought you would
get used to it if you were yelled at very young
and grow up not to mind.

(Constantly seasick, he hated being at sea,
considered the War a nuisance but did his bit.)
Finding it difficult to articulate,
one day he also told his grown-up daughter
she was not given enough love
when she was young, at least not shown.
Now he's long gone, I hear him in my head.
He gave me his power of enjoyment.
As I walk in another world from his,
over the Heath to swim in the Ladies' Pond –
how some of those Hampstead ladies
would disapprove of him in his red coat! –
in the evening I still recall the day's sights,
sounds and smells, and sometimes talk to him:
'I saw two kingfishers today.'
I recognise and love the same gusto
in his riding, roaring, as in all earth's physical
and multifariously written poetry.

Primal

Rhythm, the superabundance of God,
gusto the force by which poetry lives
begins in the guts through a pulsing cord
under the thunder in bodily caves.
First heartwork is mother's blood
beating to reach her unborn child,
upbeat, downbeat, infant food
from her substance its to build.

This is the oomph of human life,
body's generosity,
music-making love and strife,
precious, perilous energy.
No description from the baby –
neonatal verbal lack.
Heartbeat rules the memory
till the brain and nerves grow slack.

Bluebells

I wasn't very old when my father came
and took me out from boarding school
to tell me my mother was dead.
She had left him for another man,
then got ill. She wasn't happy
at the end. It was May.
We parked the car by a Devon wood
and picked a big bunch of bluebells
for her grave.
I didn't go to the funeral.
Now when I see bluebells under trees
with their sappy stems bowing
from their freight of bells
pealing a subtler scent
than their chunkier hyacinth cousins;
or when I see them in a vase,
how unhappy they are when cut,
how fast they fade,
I feel a pain in my heart.
I remember how pretty and gay she was,
the stories I heard of her courage
when we were babies in wartime Japan
(getting home to England in '42),
how effusive and ready to laugh or cry,
how they complemented, loved each other
and warmed us till things went wrong,
when she wept more and more –
'Oh, don't! Don't!' – and then died young.
Earth to earth but for me each May
she and the new bluebells are inseparable.

Gathered

Meaning organises seeing:
sensual data never neat.
Living body's complex being
answers with a learning heart.
Earth is real and it's saying
what we find and understand.
Mind and memory keep playing
heart in heart and hand in hand.

Pain confuses sweet and sharp
images as they recur.
Beauty's pleasures freshly seep
from each long-remembered flower.
Sights and sounds accumulate
more than in a single mind.
Names and poetries relate
the feeling history of our kind.

Heaven and Hell

Entwining limbs are sweet
and love is sweeter.
That one. No other.
That voice. That face.
That neck and back.
Longing in the garden.
Glimpses in the street – illusory
but reminders everywhere.
Waiting. Arrival, wine,
supper, conversation, night.
Walking in sunshine
and sitting by the river
under a dappling tree.
To have and to hold heart's desire,
be held with love.
Even when the day passes,
the taste remains forever,
confirming heaven is nowhere else
but here on earth, alive and warm
and difficult with all the complex
tenderness of plants and animals,
home, city, friends, children.

The child is ten.
The stepmother tells her:
'Better you'd never been born.
Your father wants me.
You get in the way.
When you keep crying at night
you interrupt him in bed with me.
He hates getting up.
You have no right.
You are in the wrong.'

And continues year on year:
'You bleed a lot because you're bad,
as your mother was, who bled to death.
How could anyone ever want
a mess like that?' Grown-up,
if she fails, falls out, breaks up,
she hears that high, harsh voice
crowing: 'I told you so.'
Hell is exclusion.

Heartsease

Loneliness, anxiety,
anger, disappointment haunt,
prowl like demons through the psyche,
corrode the alloy of content.
Broken cup, a jagged weapon,
stabs at random, snags and breaks
the vital web that is the human
safety net to hold mistakes.

Hatred's strong but love is stronger,
behaves more like a living plant,
that overwinters and no longer
disintegrates but sprouts if pruned.
Love opens out, exposed, may suffer
agonies of blight and loss,
yet risking it is still less bitter.
From barren ground no heartsease grows.

Pilgrim

Wrestling with God,
she found her arms
held nothing but thin air.
Afterlife evaporated too.
All had been imagination.
She still had faith, but in what?
Still felt like a pilgrim
but where was she going?

Curiously, she finds
nothing much has changed.
She still believes in goodness,
death and life
in strange strife,
the harrowing of hell,
heavenly possibilities
nowhere else but here.

Postmodernists who preach
because God's gone, so has identity –
it just floats about du-lally –
seem to her merely daft.
Though older, altered,
she's sure she's been herself
as far back as she can remember,
to about age five.

And there being no divine Nanny
to guarantee the ending,
step in and put it to bed,
doesn't mean the story's over
or there is no story. Why should it
when human authors go on writing it

with outcome anywhere
between cataclysm
or peace with justice, earthly paradise?

So at least take part,
contribute some good work
that says it for her. Not hereafter
but here and now, she wants to see.
Many times this has led her to Doubting Castle.
Why are you so full of yourself,
you piffling ant?
Why do you puff yourself up?
Aren't you just one
vanity of vanities?

On the way she is comforted
by Mr Great-Heart:
'I have often been through this Valley
and been much greater put to it than now I am.
Yet you see I am alive.'

Great-Heart

No precious five when you are dead,
no future beatific vision.
Meanwhile here on earth instead
work of seeing's never done
or the stories or the struggle
to make something not just get by,
so many and such beautiful
fellow creatures to enjoy.

Seeing with each quiet breath,
moving outward to embrace,
continue in the sight of death,
friendly, open human face.
If the sun and moon should doubt
they'd immediately go out.
Giants to fight and gloom and grief,
yet you see I am alive.

Change

But what of the broken heart?
From some catastrophes
it cannot recover.
What of the cold heart
that does not care?
What of the faint heart
that does not dare?
Let Great-Heart speak for himself
but pity the rest of us
who suffer, do harm, fail,
comply with a heartless world
that appears invincible.

It seemed so obvious,
so simple to change ourselves
and change the world, once convinced,
to do the reasonable thing,
in those more hopeful times,
with plenty still to fight for,
but confident that what was not right
could be made better.

Instead, a different era dawned
when all at once things worsened,
which lumbers on, ever more dangerous.
Dominations neuter or destroy
what gets in their way. Despair
is having a field day defeating dreams.

More complex, now in minor key,
song of experience
acknowledges responsibility,
understands that *metanoia,*

change of heart, isn't just a matter
of seeing reason – even the heart's reasons –
utters Earth's old groan for liberation,
death and life contending
in the same grand epic.

Corporate giants and hobgoblins
presume to prevail. But suddenly
in meek, unlikely places
challengers stand up to them again
to reclaim inheritance, like Managua 1979,
or in 2001, indigenous Mayans
marching from Chiapas to Mexico City –
many global foot-sloggers as well –
and humanity is not lost.

Heart of the Heartless World

Remember all the good you can,
on the way to death a love poem,
when heart of the heartless world was Spain,
Cornford's privileged spot of time.
Armed to the teeth with tenderness,
Nicaraguan pure fools
beat the odds. Now Zapatistas
show where the world's heart rules.

Heartwork means all kinds of love,
from global to most intimate,
that feed each other and believe
they overcome if they unite.
When loving more means seeing more
and seeing wants to hold the whole,
safeguard spirit, earth and air,
keep deep rhythm live and well.

2

MEXICO

MEXICO DIARY

The Dark Room

San Cristóbal de Las Casas

When I saw the room
in the small hotel
with no view of sky,
only a frosted window
onto a corridor
it seemed full of gloom.
Clean with a private shower,
it was good value but felt like a cell.
I thought, I'll stay here tonight
then move. The strange noises
grew quiet. I slept.

When I opened my door
and saw the new sunshine
dapple the courtyard
next morning I started to mellow.
I wandered the city for days
through bright dusty streets.
I went into many dark buildings
that opened all of a sudden to sunlit
quadrangles brilliant with flowers.
One had a scarlet bougainvillea
at least twenty feet high.

When I got back to my room
I did not mind its twilight,
as I lay on the bed exhausted.
Slowly the red, the blue,
the green, the yellow shapes

appeared unbidden in my head
until consciousness slid away.
Out of the apparently sterile,
prosaic, murky medium,
sharp images floated delicately
as unforgettable perfume.

The Beautiful Game

At Palenque and Tenem Puente,
ruined Mayan palaces
I saw the still preserved *pelota*
courts for their ritual ball game.
I could not discover whether
it was the winners or the losers
who were sacrificed.

Back at my hotel, Alejandro,
the young Mexican at reception
(teacher-training student in the mornings),
was absorbed in the football on TV.
I asked him: 'Do you remember
Maradona aided by the hand of God?'
'Yes,' he said, he did.

Angry gods of grain
destroyed triumphant Gazza
and I thought of Southgate's face
when he lost the penalty
known as sudden death.

Confirmation

At Grutas de Rancho Nuevo
the huge caves of pinkish rock
go on and on. Figures emerge
half-formed human or animal
amid the dripping stalagmites and stalactites.

The dark river runs below.
It is a journey into the imagination
of the poet Coleridge.
Here chasms tumble deeper far
than any he had seen in Somerset.
He should have come to Mexico.

At Palenque one of the Mayan temples
is named after a German count
who in the early nineteenth century
made his home in it.
What a pity that he never
invited Coleridge to dinner.

How strange for the poet to discover
that what he had imagined actually was there,
as for his modern reader
to encounter forms familiar
from his English shaping spirit,
still existing, now as then abroad,
before and after him, themselves,
measureless caverns, jungle palaces,
not in his poetry but in the world.

Grandeur

I sat and stared for more than half an hour
at the huge waterfall of Agua Azul
I saw two giant figures inside it,
standing side by side,
the male and female genius of the place
in constant motion but always there,
because they were made of water.

On another trip, this time
with a tough, articulate old lady,
housewifely Mexican Catholic,
joyriding on holiday from her family
alone, having ignored all their objections,
at every scenic marvel she exclaimed:
¡La grandeza de Dios!
How great is God's grandeur!

A routinely pious litany
but then, I thought, it's her vocabulary
for the power of a place she feels,
and not so far removed
from pagan, pantheist,
or even godless lover of the Earth,
something far more deeply interfused
or the Mayan gods of nature
her predecessors persecuted
so fanatically but failed to conquer.

Seat

Zócalo, San Cristóbal de Las Casas

The Zócalo is the main square of this city,
which gives a clear sense of itself,
comprehensible as you can walk anywhere.
There are palm trees in these gardens
behind low, curly iron railings
painted green. A flock of indigenous children
sell coloured woven belts and small clay animals.
Sheeny raucous grackles form a loud bird chorus
with a plethora of sparrows
chattering in Mexican in warm dust baths –
emigrants perhaps from London.

For a Londoner in February
it is a pleasant place to sit
on a green bench with backrest wrought
with the founder's arms, Conquistador
Diego de Mazariegos, 1528.
The rotunda bandstand in the middle
has two levels – the top for music
and under it a café with a terrace
all the way round. Again the railings
are painted green and the matching iron chairs
elaborately wrought with the new
conquering logo, Coca Cola.

This city with such talent and appetite
for all that is sweet in life
wants to enjoy itself
in sunny peace but even here
is branded by the iron lords
that have never left it sitting comfortably.

Zapatistas Retake San Cristóbal de Las Casas

February 24ᵗʰ 2001

Tonight the Zapatistas retake San Cristóbal.
Tzotzil, Tzeltal, Zoque, Chol
and Tojolabal march in
from their villages in uplands,
valleys and the jungle of Lacandon.
The name of one is *La Realidad:* Reality.

Some are masked with paisley handkerchiefs,
others with home-made balaclavas,
often with pom-pom bobbles on the top.
The woven and embroidered clothes
the women wear are brilliant
as their native flowers and birds.
Some use their shawls as slings
to carry babies on their backs.

Distinguished men have crowned their knitted masks
with ceremonial hats of woven straw
and many-coloured ribbons floating down.
Adolescents have fashioned paper headbands,
round which they have written:
PEACE WITH DIGNITY.
Some have no shoes, all are unarmed.
They are smiling, singing and shouting slogans:
Zapata vive. La lucha sigue.
Viva Civil Society! Viva!

When they took the City Hall in 1994,
Marcos reported that tourists asked him
if they could take photographs.
With his dry sense of humour he replied:

'Excuse me, but this is a Revolution!'
None was harmed.

Swollen like the Grijalva River after rain –
a Chiapan tribe jumped into it and drowned
when finally defeated by conquistadors –
seven years on the Zapatistas now
flood in their thousands onto the Cathedral Square,
where *Señora* Civil Society
(thus addressed in countless communiqués
'from the South-East Mexican mountains'),
has been waiting patiently all day
until, late at night, the 23 comandantes –
4 are women – mount the platform
and last to speak for 'us who are earth-coloured'
is Marcos, their *sub*-comandante.

Next morning in the foggy chill
sleepy groups huddle round camp fires,
where they have spent the night,
then regather in strength
along the main road to Tuxtla
for the next lap of their caravan
to Mexico City, once Tenochtitlán.

Poor they are, but force of the forgotten heart
whose homeliest reasons cannot be denied,
today they are swelling as a song
with strange polyphonous global resonance,
for a world with room for many worlds,
for themselves, their fellow creatures and the Earth
they know as common mother of us all.

3

PEOPLE AND OCCASIONS

For Arnold

On his Eightieth Birthday – 2001

You see all you struggled for
so long, so hard recede.
Unbetraying still, but saddened yes,
you have made it to the millennium
but will not enter the promised land
you gazed on fresh in the sun below.

All March through
the sun hid its face for shame.
The diseased country is closed.
Weeping eyes are stung by smoke
from pyres of slaughtered animals
with helpless obtruding legs.

And still so many children poor.
TB increases in a rich nation
now too mean to ensure enough
serum to inoculate them all.
Passengers are killed on railways,
like so much else, falling apart.

England hosts a patent protection summit
while AIDS decimates Africa.
Bush reneges on Kyoto
defending the right of 'Americans'
to poison the sick Earth,
on and on, even to the death.

The Idol that rules the world,
manufactured of silver and gold,
insists on its daily diet of sacrifice.

It has no heart. Its hands don't feel.
Its ears don't hear. Its eyes can't see.
It does not cry from its throat.

This hobgoblin *can* daunt the spirit.
Is all heart lost? In 1936
the heart of the heartless world
was Spain, Cornford on the last mile
to Huesca cried, 'Remember
all the good you can.'

In 1979 Nicaragua reached
for the moon. 'The moon was the Earth
our bit of Earth and we got there.
And now Rugama,
it's beginning to belong to the poor,
the Earth is, with its moon.'

Rugama, like Cornford a poet
killed aged 20, was one of the 50,000
who died for that. And Borge's revenge
on his torturers was to give their children
schools, and them his hand they had ill-treated
with all its tenderness intact.

Now defeat follows defeat and the ever
more arrogant Ideology
claims it is unassailable.
But then again out of the remote
jungle of Lacandon
News from Somewhere and at hand.

This February I saw the Zapatistas
pour into San Cristóbal
at the start of their long march,

to the capital, Mexico City,
for living, indigenous, ordinary
people against the golden Idol.

These are the forgotten heart
who suddenly appear
and the heartless world can still
take heart from them. And you,
Arnold, are part of that cry
as a poet who can hear and see and say,

witness to what the Idol cannot do.
You are among the 144 thousand
who have not bent the knee.
You too have sown seeds
in the soil of language,
a crop for us from small immediate things.

You may feel your seeds and poems
have been a small part of the action
but they remain where the heart is,
belong with the best, where small
human beings battle against a Beast
so huge it respects nothing at all.

To Tony van der Poorten

Autumn deluded the grass
on Clapham Common
to grow as in the spring,
vivid as a green parrot,
and the flame colours
creeping through the trees
seemed to add extra energy.
So many visitors walked this way
to see you in the hospice

When I first came
you too were fierily alive,
and lucid as the blue October sky.
From your bed you master-minded
all the details of Ofelia's meeting –
leaflets, mailshots, bossed us all about.
I learned more about the things you'd done
We had long talks about your native Sri Lanka,
Mexico, printing, the future.

Straight from the press
I brought you my translation,
dedicated to you,
of Marcos' *Zapatista Stories*.
You were overjoyed and wept:
'No one has ever dedicated a book
to me before,' you said.
'It's been my life. It's been my life.'
Your own fierce dedication was encouragement.

The last time I saw you,
you were wandering away
and now you've gone.

Now your ashes will nourish
the soil of Belize,
become food for the trees
where indigenous parrots fly
and indigenous peoples
strive to live free.

You'll become earth of our Earth
where humanity's multiple worlds
have their only home. As this planet
turns more years round the sun,
through London autumn and spring,
tropical rain and dry season,
you will be present in many minds
as part of the fabric of hope,
not of delusion.

The Old Campaigner

The old campaigner still keeps on the go.
He is as prickly as a roving bramble,
he's difficult but yet we love him so.

He turns up everywhere, is in the know.
He does not hurry as he likes to amble.
The old campaigner still keeps on the go.

His lengthy rhetoric will ebb and flow,
epigrammatic but prefers to ramble.
He's difficult but yet we love him so.

On every march for justice he will show,
in gnomic woolly hat you'll see him shamble.
The old campaigner still keeps on the go.

He's open-hearted, kind to friend and foe
but when his rage may boil is just a gamble.
He's difficult but yet we love him so.

Year in, year out, in sun, in rain, in snow,
it's that old anarchic wimble wamble.
The old campaigner still keeps on the go,
he's difficult but yet we love him so.

Hoddesdon Wood

For David Perman

Between twisty oaks in the goblin wood
sunlight shimmers a greenish haze.
The host of lichened trunks thrust up
to the mild March day's blue sky.
Across them afternoon shadows curl
in mirror warp that darkly weaves
even more magical density through
their contorted, bare, still dance.

I sit on a velvet mossy stump,
at my feet crackle brittle leaves,
brown like the bracken of the forest floor.
Bird calls point the flow of quiet
they tell is bringing the spring, the outburst
whose signs I saw preparing on my way –
stray clump of early primroses,
cone-laden larch sprouting afresh.

I feel the power. I wait to write.
From childhood it has visited and withdrawn.
The seeing is transitory and as I've grown
I've spelt it differently. No longer God.
Call it bliss, loneliness seeking union
love instressing insight pouring out
what I can say now from where I am
in a language that is mine and yours.

To a Friend

For Anne

Country houses are cold in winter.
A Londoner now for years,
I have grown soft and wait for warmth
before I revisit those out of town.
June: railway banks and hedgerows
overflow with dog roses, modest
and delicate native flower, blushing
to deepest pink, paling to bridal white.
But it rained all week, everything overgrown,
fierce nettles threatened on every footpath.
You had to laugh when I kept
dripping back into your kitchen,
drenched through yet again.

Disappointing. But we did get to the sea
and I saw with my eyes of another summer
your Suffolk cliffs, hillocks, heather,
oaks, orchids, marshes, swans with cygnets,
that refresh the fabric of the mind
preoccupied amid the fretful stir.
('They folks be mad in London –
always rushing about,' as I heard
a sheep farmer say on Exmoor.)

But even more as we sat indoors
and lightning cracked and thunder roared,
what I will treasure is our conversation,
a squirrel store of provisions
for the dark teatimes. What I will hoard
is the luxury of knowing and being known –
everyday face to face – not the whole

ocean but many approaching
deep and shallow winding waters.
Heaven's promised transparency
of beatific vision matters less to me
than a friend found on earth like you
gently in time by slow disclosure.

Garden

For Michael

'Your husband doesn't like gardening, does he?'
someone in the village told your wife.
Meaning your huge garden is wild
with a will of its own. It is full
of plants you brought back from your travels
and rare trees, many grown from seed,
commingle with the common to distinguish
the wide skyline, windbreak
from storms off the North Sea
and over the flat Suffolk fields.

This was the year of the foxgloves rampant,
some taller than us, some purple,
some paler or even white and dappled
with delicate markings in their open mouths.
You pointed out what was planted
in the beds round your meadow lawn
and we wrestled through your marsh and orchard,
more overgrown than ever after so much rain.
Like every countryman, you grumbled about the weather
and all the work that needed to be done.

I saw the mulberry which the hurricane had felled
and left with its roots in the air,
now recumbent, firmly re-rooted,
flourishing among honesty and Himalayan balsam.
I thought, despite your Berlin origin
and childhood escape from Nazi Germany,
how well you too were rooted here.

I felt how palpably you loved this earth,
by making a garden thrive that had become,
like you, both very English and extraordinary.

Minutes From Home

Camden Town Station is agitated,
grimy and full of strangers.
Sainsbury's bewilders me
and I forget to get butter.
I cross with a crowd at the lights,
which take ages to change
and the traffic roars on.
Heaving my carrier bags, I weave
through the fidgety, fixed-gaze
queues at the bus stops.

At last I come to St Martin's Gardens
and stroll through the playground
where I know the children,
into the ease of my street.
I turn to face the afternoon light,
gold through the trees at the end.
The family at number fourteen
are sitting outside in their saris.
'Hullo,' call the mothers
in their turtle dove voices
and the two smallest girls,
proud of their beautiful dresses,
wave and grin.

'All right?' shouts Dave
sitting on his wall with a beer,
after painting his front door again
(about once a month). I praise the colour.
'All right, Dinah?' Elsie reiterates,
'I've just been watering Kate's flowers.'
Kate is well over eighty
and her husband fought in Spain.

Later I may sit out with Elsie
and hear the gossip. She misses nothing.
It is her pleasure to be chronicler of sagas,
narrator who is a character in the story.
'Them squirrels are a blinking nuisance,'
she says, but loves cats and small birds,
watches the opening of every flower.
She disapproves of my buddleia
and time after time she gently suggests
a nice clematis or a climbing rose.
I think she will win.

But for now I go indoors,
put the kettle on, make tea,
settle on the sofa
with Dapple purring beside me,
home in my head and my skin.

Mario

Mario sings, 'I am the boom, the boom!'
He clasps the mike and croons, stripped to the waist,
'Oh, big it up for Mario, he's the best!'
Great cat of cats his caterwauling room
now swells through windows open flung to street
and all the wicked glamour of the world.
Though London's cat-laced, neighbours are appalled
but Mario has his gang and life is sweet.
He swaggers out with his new rock star walk.
Of late he cultivates a slight moustache,
a chubby teenage truant on the town.
Leading small vandal sorties is his work.
He can barely read or write, defies the harsh
awakening if his dream-life lets him down.

Faithless

I peeped through downstairs window and I saw
you extended on the futon in delight,
pleased with yourself and where you'd spent the night
with a companion ready to adore.
She was Japanese and elegant and more
your age than me. With you she lay there quite
oblivious of my rage. For hours she might
just read her book and stroke you on the floor.
A furious drudge I trudge to buy your food,
unload my trolley thoroughly aggrieved,
lay fish in fridge and stocks of cupboard love.
In dark I wake, descend in mellowed mood
for milk, still of your yellow eyes bereaved.
You come to me purring like an angel dove.

Cosmic

For Helen

At supper in the evening garden,
sunset of a warm summer's day,
fresh after weeks of dull green rain,
we looked up to the flat roof
of the bathroom back addition
and saw one small black leaf
peeping over it. It twitched –
it was Dapple the cat's ear.

I remembered how at school
we used to laugh at the hymn line:
'O give me Samuel's ear,'
and here was the cat's, somehow
equally comical. I don't aspire
to apprehend Yahweh whistling in the dark.
This was the reverse, it twitched again,
an animal vegetable mineral ear
listening to us: what are we humans
up to?

As night came down and we lit a candle,
with several empty bottles on the table,
we told secrets, murmured hurts and desires.
Now bemused by a bird it had heard,
in the long grass the cat sat rigid.
Out of the vast pre-verbal cosmos
entrusted to curious talking creatures,
its luminous yellow eyes stared at us.

Kind

For Zoe

On Sundays you often come to tea,
entertaining a grateful mother.
One afternoon: 'What kind of bird is that?'
you asked. I wasn't sure –
a small brown speckled,
still quite fluffy one.
Was it a wren or a baby sparrow?

Next afternoon I watched it
pecking at the earth beside a robin.
Slightly at first, it began
to get robin habits – cocked its head,
bobbed about, tick tick alarm,
puffed up its chest feathers
faintly pinkening like the dawn.

As you kindly visit my garden plum-tree –
releasing a responding trill
of kindness for my human part –
each day you become more clearly
an individual of the robin kind.

Horns

For Tom

We went to Richmond Park to look for deer,
your sister hadn't been since she was five,
on a picnic, when one butted her
and knocked her down.
We walked far, thought we were out of luck.
But you seemed to have an affinity,
suddenly you pointed to what appeared
to be branches poking out of the bracken.
Drawing near we saw sixteen big red stags.
You told us how a king would put on antlers
and run wild at Beltane. In the oak forest
you stretched your arms across one mighty girth,
impossible to encompass it.

I remember you playing the coaching horn
at your grandfather's memorial,
how you had to stand in the porch
because they thought the instrument
too pagan to play in church,
but in that same country church a few years on
you did play your trumpet
for your uncle who died young.
You marked the ending with a great parp.
Then I think of all the times you play
on jollier, Brightonic occasions when people dance.
Kingly stags, Beltane rites, branching oaks,
your arms, your fingers, all your feeling range
mix into the most ancient music.

The Ash Tree

For Anne Mieke

You read my typescript
and anxiously you telephone to tell me
Ygdrasil was not a sycamore:
it was an ash.
Will that invalidate the poem?
I reassure you I already knew
my dear sycamore in Camden Town
wasn't the original world tree.
I just named it after it,
as if, had your parents called you Mary,
they probably didn't mean you are
God's mother, Queen of Heaven.
Your Dutch soul gives a little shudder,
then you laugh, relieved.

The ash, you continue, used to be revered
because the same tree may bear
both male and female flowers,
be in itself the doubleness
that weaves and holds our world.
I walk out in April, May to look at it.
I feel its bark, smooth grey or calmly rippling,
note the sooty, deer-footed buds,
then blackish male clumps, almost like caviar
and the lengthening female petal bunches
that will become the keys.
With these still in bloom the first leaves
frill out from the extremities
of upward urging, arching twiggy branches.

And I am thankful
you are such a good artist
because you observe so minutely,
care about every particular
with your Low-Country respect
for nature's matter of fact,
that issues in protest at what is threatened
and your passionate compositions –
your green secular spirit absorbing,
transforming the positive energy
from fierce old Nordic sagas
and Ometeotl, Aztec supreme
Lord and Lady of Duality.

For George and Katherine

At Your Silver Wedding Party
12th September 1998

Twenty-five years have passed
since we went to your wedding.
I remember Father, still dapper then
and with an air of playing hooky,
arriving by helicopter and leaping down
onto the field, followed by the pilot,
who swept off her helmet
and shook out her long blond hair
like a scene from James Bond.

I remember Tom and Zoe
your nephew and niece
both here tonight and taller than me now
but then small children, entranced
to be whisked up on their first flight.
That was quite a wedding
and you the bridegroom and bride
looked so pleased with yourselves
you had made it, as well you might.

Twenty five years have passed;
Your sons are six-foot men.
Here tonight: Edward, handsome
with a look of Katherine
and Max your youngest is twenty-one
and sharing your party. He is athletic,
with gentle manners and a good mind.
You can be proud to have made
your quarter century,
quite an achievement these transient days.

I have watched you, George,
who used to bark out orders
with a touch of the sergeant major,
mellow under Katherine's delicate care,
broaden your scope to study –
with a hefty thesis – how to be fit past fifty,
yourself, and the rest of us old codgers.

I have watched you, Katherine,
holding your job in design
together with house and family,
so efficient, so self-effacing
expert at so many crafts and cooking,
your mince pies and Christmas cake
the best we ever tasted
and we have enjoyed them each year;
you so skilled at making people comfortable
not just at home. Not long ago
when I visited you in hospital
you were ill but you made me welcome
and I realised later I had told you
all my troubles about the terrible lodgers
I had at the time.
Your quietness is the courage
to keep going. Softly softly
you are tough and firm.

I think George is lucky
to have you for a wife.
You are lucky to have each other.
Now you have stuck it out this far
to your silver wedding party,

I wish you for the future
a long and happy life together.
Keep fit, keep going, keep heart
and be full of adventures and pleasure.

Birdman

The assistant birdman of Regent's Park
says he lives out in the sticks
in a village just past Watford.
In the morning he walks more than a mile
to the station to catch the 5.38 into Euston.
He wears paddling shorts showing hairy legs
and knobbly knees. Taken rather aback
by his Cockney-on-the-Costa physique,
a Hampstead couple with expensive binoculars
quiz him about his qualifications.

'When the job came up
my mate that works here
he knew I were a birder,
said why don't I go for it like
and well, I got it.'

He knows every bird in the park
to the feathers they add with the years.
A bleeper at his belt records sightings
of rare specimens elsewhere in England.
In the middle of the playing fields
he scans the sky and in sudden ecstasy
exclaims: 'Osprey! Osprey!'
With his whole body intending upward,
radiance streams from his face
like an angel.

Regent's Park is in the middle of a big city
and not near the river. These are just
some of the birds to be seen in it:
Great crested grebe, Leache's petrel,
gannet, cormorant, shag, little egret,

grey heron, Whooper swan, mute swan, spoonbill,
red crested pochard, pintail, garganey,
mallard, shelduck, greylag goose,
widgeon, mandarin, gadwall, teal,
goldeneye, honey buzzard, kestrel, smew,
sparrowhawk, hen harrier, merlin, moorhen,
pheasant, grey partridge, corncrake, peregrine,
shoveler, oystercatcher, lapwing, coot,
whimbrel, woodpigeon, bar-tailed godwit,
golden plover, stone curlew, dunlin, snipe,
wryneck, herring gull, kittiwake, tern,
green woodpecker, woodlark, skylark, wren,
guillemot, turtle dove, barn owl, cuckoo,
sand martin, tawny pipit, ring ouzel, stonechat,
greater spotted woodpecker, kingfisher, swift,
sedge warbler, whitethroat, blackcap, chiffchaff,
carrion crow, yellowhammer, chaffinch, brambling,
song thrush, mistle thrush, fieldfare, firecrest,
nightingale, blackbird, dunnock, robin,
bullfinch, goldfinch, sparrow, siskin,
treecreeper, linnet, jackdaw, jay,
blue tit, great tit, red breasted flycatcher,
long tailed tit, nuthatch, great grey shrike,
greenshank, sandpiper, hobby, woodcock,
pied wagtail, yellow wagtail, magpie, rook.

Here beginneth the Parliament of Fowls:
The life so short the craft so long to learn,
th'assay so hard, so sharp the conquerring . . .

And when this work all brought was to an ende,
to every foul Nature gave his make,
by even accord and on their way they wende
and Lord, the blisse and joye that they make!